WHY CAN'T

DO THAT?

This Book Belongs To

With special thanks to

Jane Foulkes, Louise Bomber and Mica Douglas

Published by

B3long

Central Boulevard

Blythe Valley Business Park

Solihull

B90 8AG

01564 711019

www.b3long.co.uk

Text copyright © F Newood 2011

Illustrations copyright © G Newood 2013

First Published 2014

All rights reserved. The whole of this work, including all text and illustrations, is protected by copyright. No part of this work may be loaded, stored, manipulated, reproduced or transmitted in any form or by any means, electronic or mechanical, including photocopying and recording or by any information storage and retrieval system without prior knowledge and written permission from the publisher, on behalf of the copyright owners.

This book is a work of fiction. Names, characters, businesses, organizations, places and events are either a product of the author's imagination or are used fictitiously. Any resemblance to actual persons, living or dead, events or locales is entirely coincidental.

ISBN: 978-0-9926629-0-5

Foreword

Children and young people who have experienced significant relational traumas and losses are at high risk of being misunderstood and misinterpreted. Why Can't I Do That? is a significant read for a time such as this that will resonate not only with the children who sit alongside grown-ups curious about Little Ben, but also with those grown-ups who are often too quick to judge behaviours, too busy or naive to understand what is really being communicated. This book slows the reader down, allowing opportunity to consider both the shared developmental vulnerabilities around for children and young people such as this, and highlighting the amazing potential for brain development.

Created together with Fi and Gail Newood's own children, Switches brings hope to those out there confused and even despairing of why they do what they do. These children and young people are not stupid. They know intrinsically that they are different to their peers. They experience this difference day in, day out – at home, at school, in their communities. Surely it is time now that we got alongside them to honour that difference with the understanding and respect deserved.

History shows that a little understanding goes a long way. Adopted child, Apple founder and shaper of culture, Steve Jobs, was one of those children. Widely seen as a troublemaker rather than as a special child, one particular teacher, Imogen Hill, recognised Jobs' potential and worked with him in a way that honoured and respected his difference.

If we only realised the significance of getting alongside the Little Bens of this world we could optimise more of the moment-by-moment opportunities to impact these young lives. The fragile self would stand taller as hope and dignity were rightfully claimed. Who knows what could be possible with a deeper level of understanding. The makings of another Steve Jobs maybe? This fantastic book shows that there is treasure to unlock, or 'switch on', in each and every child.

Louise Michelle Bomber – Attachment Support Teacher Therapist

About the Authors

Fi has been working with Looked After Children for 13 years, initially in residential settings but for past five years as a Therapeutic Foster Parent. She is a qualified life coach, trainer, has studied Therapeutic Fostering at degree level and is currently doing an MA in Integrative Counselling and Psychotherapy.

Fi is interested in the role of the adult in supporting young people to maturity, the impact of abuse, trauma and neglect on the developing brain and the practical ways theories and research can be used to support the child.

"Young people respond best to a relationship-focused rather than child-centred service. To best meet the needs of the young person we also have to consider those of the parent or professional working or living with them. It is by understanding our own histories, relationships, needs and wishes that we can best support the young person with theirs".

Gail is a JNC Degree qualified Youth worker with over 26 years of experience in both the statutory and voluntary sector. She is a qualified mentor, CAF lead, sexual health advisor, foster parent and youth participation lead.

Gail's interests lie in ensuring that young people's voices are truly heard and in moving them forward to a better understanding of themselves, others and their place in society.

"A young person's sense of worth is shaped by the communities they inhabit. So if their home or school community is broken so too are they. It's important not to just cover over their brokenness but to truly enable them to mend themselves".

Together Fi and Gail are the founders of

B3long Therapeutic Youth Service (www.b3long.co.uk)

For our children,

Hayden, Shane and Scott.

Your switches amaze us daily.

We love you.

When Little Ben came down for breakfast he had a feeling that today was not going to be a good day. In fact Little Ben could not remember the last time he had had a good day. Little Ben felt like he was always doing things wrong and never got anything right.

Every morning there was a rush for Little Ben's foster mum to get him and his sister ready for school. Little Ben was always the last one to finish breakfast, the last one to use the bathroom and the last one to get dressed. Little Ben took so long to do these things that he never got the chance to play before school.

Why can't I do that? Little Ben thought to himself. I'm such a slow-coach.

As soon as he arrived at school Little Ben had assembly. Little Ben wasn't allowed to sit with the rest of his class, he had to sit next to his teacher Mrs Fieldhouse. Assemblies always felt like they went on forever. Little Ben liked the singing but he found it hard to sit still and concentrate and he was always being told to be quiet. Little Ben looked around and noticed how all the other children were quiet and listening hard.

Why can't I do that? Little Ben thought to himself. I'm such a fidget pants.

After assembly Little Ben had literacy. Normally he liked getting to hear stories but today Mrs Fieldhouse was in a really bad mood. Little Ben couldn't work out what he was doing wrong but he knew it had to be him because the other children were always good.

When Mrs Fieldhouse shouted at the class to be quiet Little Ben felt scared and thought he was going to cry. The other children didn't seem to worry though and just got on with their work.

Why can't I do that? Little Ben thought to himself. I'm such a baby.

Next it was lunchtime. Little Ben hated lunchtime. He always tried to get into the lunch hall first but then he would watch all of the other children come in and know that no-one would sit on his table until all of the other tables were full.

Today Little Ben looked around and saw all his classmates grouped together eating and sharing their food.

Why can't I do that? Little Ben thought to himself. No-one will ever like me.

After he'd eaten little Ben went out to play. Now that he was in junior school Little Ben wasn't allowed to use the play equipment like the infant school children were. Juniors were expected to come up with their own games but Little Ben found this very difficult. He tried to join in with some older children who were playing tag but they just laughed at him and ran away.

In the end Little Ben went and sat alone and watched all the other children playing and laughing together.

Why can't I do that? thought Little Ben to himself. I'll never have any friends.

In the afternoon was maths. When Mrs Fieldhouse put the sums up on the board Little Ben quickly wrote the first one down. He tried to answer it but it was very hard. He was going to put his hand up and ask for help but he saw that all the other children were busy writing their answers.

Why can't I do that? Little Ben thought to himself. I'm just stupid.

So, he threw his book onto the floor and his teacher sent him out of the room.

At the end of the day Little Ben's mum came to collect him from school and she spent some time with Mrs Fieldhouse discussing his day. Little Ben wasn't allowed to hear what they were saying but he knew that his teacher was telling his Mum about all of the bad things he had done.

Little Ben watched as the other children ran out of school, greeted their parents and left without ever needing to see the teachers.

Why can't I do that? thought Little Ben to himself.
I'm so naughty.

The day didn't seem to get any better for Little Ben when he got home either. He found it hard to share his toys with his sister and took ages to get his homework done.

After dinner, when he was supposed to be doing the washing up, he managed to flood the kitchen floor!

Little Ben thought his mum was going to be really mad with him and tried hard to clean up the mess but she caught him.

Mum asked Little Ben to come and sit with her on the sofa. "I think you are trying to let me know that today has been such a hard day for you and that you are feeling very wobbly inside" said Mum.

"I thought that instead of a story tonight maybe I could tell you about your switches and maybe it will help you to understand why things can be so hard for you".

Little Ben was relieved that his Mum wasn't cross about the kitchen floor. He felt a lot better knowing that she wanted to help him and he agreed that he wanted to know about switches.

"Your brain is very, very clever" said Mum. "It's like millions of switches all joined together. For everything you do there's a switch. There's a switch for laughing, a switch for jumping and a switch for riding a bike."

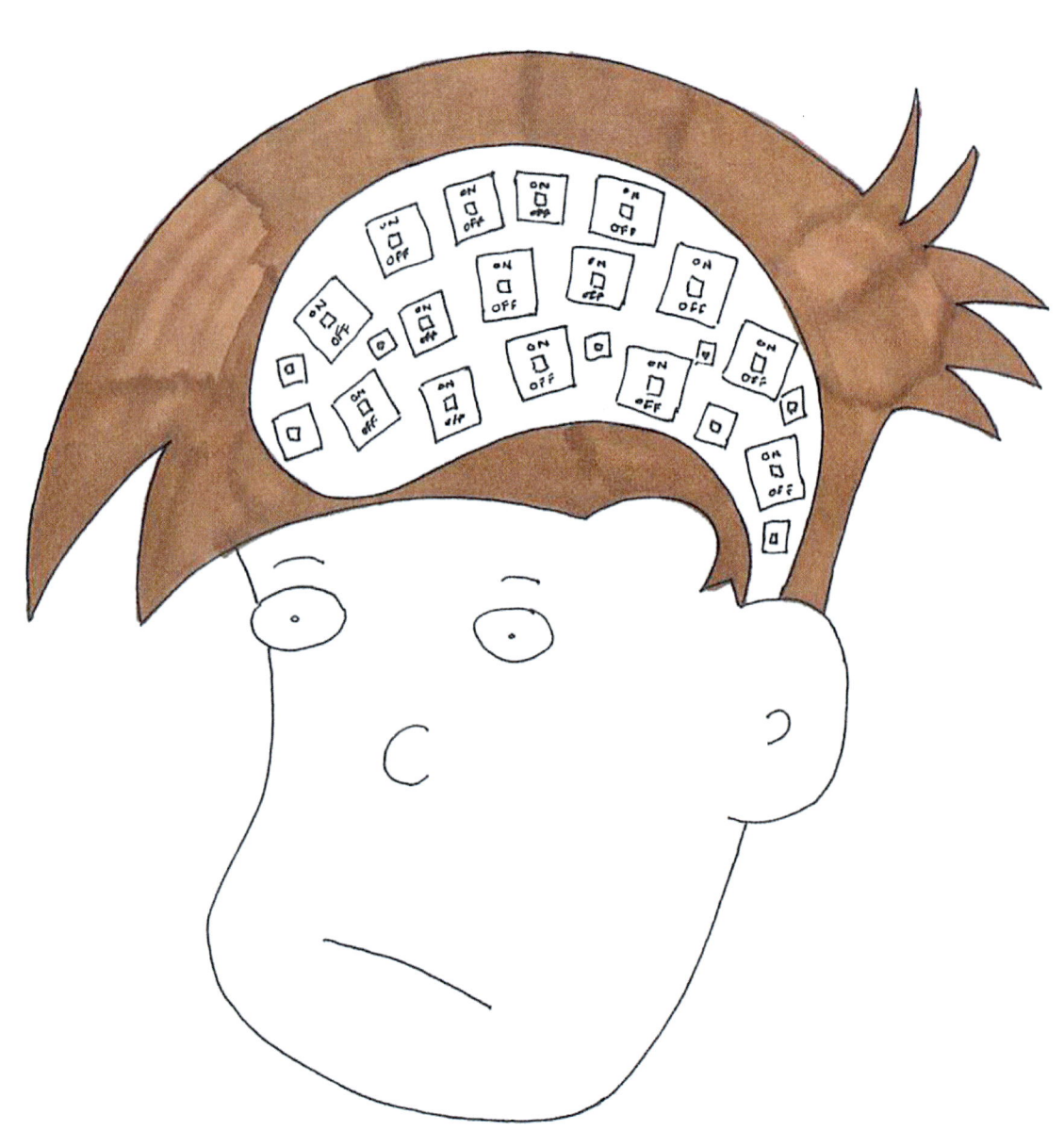

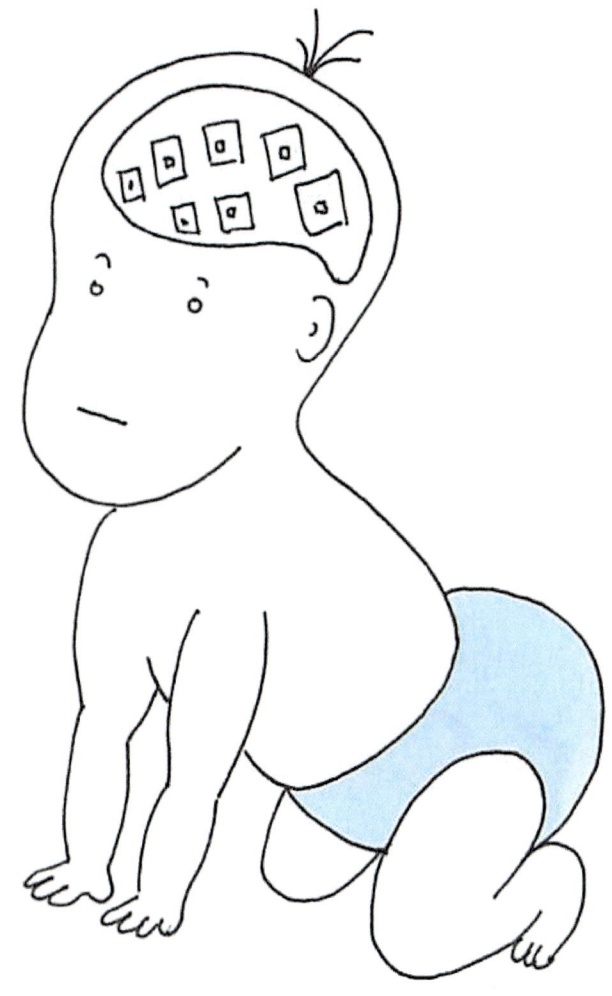

"When a baby is born they know how to breathe and how to cry if they want something but nearly all of their other switches are turned off. A baby cannot turn its switches on by itself, it's too hard, so as the baby grows into a child the parents help them turn their switches on at the right times. Some switches come on very quickly, others take time and some flicker on and off for a while."

"For some parents turning on switches is very difficult. They might not know how to turn them on or they might turn the wrong ones on at the wrong time.

If your switches aren't turned on properly then sometimes they end up getting stuck. That might make you feel really different to other children.

If your learning switch is stuck then you might think you're stupid. If your playing nicely switch is stuck then you might find it hard to make friends. If your concentrating switch is stuck then you might find it hard to sit still and listen."

"Where is your brain?" asked Mum.

Little Ben tapped his head.

Can you see it? Mum asked him.

"No" Little Ben replied.

"Well, this is the problem with switches" said Mum. "If people can't see them then they might not understand that some of them are stuck. They might think you can do things that are really very hard for you.

"The good news though is that your switches can become unstuck. Some may turn on easily, some may spend time flickering on and off and some may need a lot of work.

If you want I can help you with your switches?"

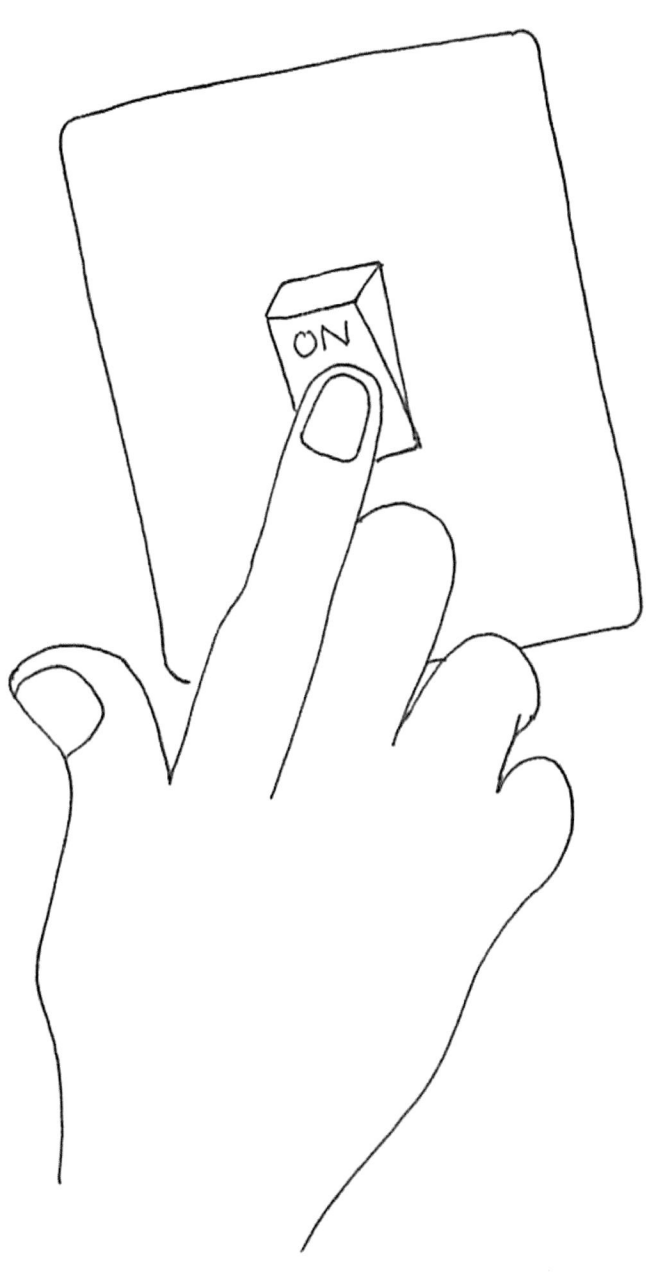

Ben nodded and smiled. Now that he knew about switches he understood why he felt so different to the other children.

He wasn't a baby, stupid or naughty. He just needed some more help and his mum was going to give it to him.

Ben felt so happy and couldn't wait to see which switch would turn on first.

Switches I Would Like Help With

....

....

....

....

....

....

....

....